BY JOE TOUGAS

PRESIDENT KENNEDY'S KILLER AND THE AMERICA HE LEFT BEHIND

THE ASSASSIN, THE CRIME, AND THE END OF A HOPEFUL VISION IN CHAOTIC TIMES

COMPASS POINT BOOKS
a capstone imprint

With love to my mother and proud Kennedy supporter, Mary Tougas —JT

Assassins' America is published by Compass Point Books, a Capstone imprint
1710 Roe Crest Drive, North Mankato, Minnesota 56003
www.mycapstone.com

Library of Congress Cataloging-in-Publication Data
Names: Tougas, Joe, author.
Title: President Kennedy's killer and the America he left behind : the assassin, the crime, and the end of a hopeful vision in chaotic times / by Joe Tougas.
Description: North Mankato, Minnesota : Compass Point Books, 2018. |
Series: Assassins' America | Audience: Ages 9-15.
Identifiers: LCCN 2017042671 (print) | LCCN 2017043546 (ebook) |
ISBN 9780756557218 (eBook pdf) | ISBN 9780756557133 (hardcover) |
ISBN 9780756557171 (pbk.)
Subjects: LCSH: Kennedy, John F. (John Fitzgerald), 1917-1963—Assassination—Juvenile literature. | Oswald, Lee Harvey—Juvenile literature.
Classification: LCC E842.9 (ebook) | LCC E842.9 .T68 2018 (print) |
DDC 973.922092—dc23
LC record available at https://lccn.loc.gov/2017042671

Editorial Credits
Nick Healy, editor; Mackenzie Lopez and Kay Fraser, designers; Svetlana Zhurkin, media researcher; Tori Abraham, production specialist

Printed and bound in the United States of America.
010749S18

TABLE OF CONTENTS

President John F. Kennedy

CHAPTER 1
A PROMISING PRESIDENT

It's a storied name, Kennedy. It's a name that rings of an exciting time of change in American history and of incredible, unbelievable tragedy. It's a name that recalls a famous family that in many ways was the closest the United States ever came to having royalty. The Kennedys were a wealthy clan with many children, some of whom became powerful Americans. One of them became president of the United States.

Famous and glamorous and seen as heroic, the Kennedys captured the country's imagination. And when he became president, John F. Kennedy asked his fellow Americans to use their imaginations, challenging them to "ask not what your country can do for you, but what you can do for your country."

Young, witty, and handsome, John F. Kennedy was a new kind of president for the time, and according to some historians, he was an effective and promising president — possibly a great one.

He was the second son of Rosemary Fitzgerald and Joseph P. Kennedy, a pair who met at the beginning of the 20th century in Maine. Joe, a Harvard University graduate, was at age 25 the youngest bank president in the world. From the day she was born, Rosemary Fitzgerald lived a fairy-tale life of riches and respect in Boston. Rosemary's father, nicknamed "Honey" Fitzgerald, served as a member of Congress for three terms, then worked as a newspaper publisher before running successfully for mayor of Boston. The family was so rich and powerful, in fact, that they at first didn't want Rosemary to get all that comfy with the young banker, Joseph Kennedy. They didn't think he was good enough for their daughter.

But Joe and Rosemary didn't care. Their two families could only stand by and watch as the two fell in love and married in 1914. Their family began growing shortly afterward, starting with the birth of Joseph Jr. and, two years later, of John Fitzgerald. He was born May 29, 1917, in an upstairs bedroom of a two-and-a-half story house in Boston. Around the time of John's birth, his father left banking and moved into the steel industry, then into stockbroking. He made millions of dollars. The family grew as his fortunes did, and eventually the Kennedys had nine children.

Growing up, John Fitzgerald Kennedy was known as "Jack." Like his mother, he enjoyed many of the spoils that come with a rich upbringing. There were maids, nurses, and a big family. Kennedy would later describe it as "an easy, prosperous life."

He liked to compete, and he competed with nobody more than his older brother, Joseph Jr. The two would fight frequently, with Jack frustrated by his older brother's athletic edge. They

Joseph and Rose Kennedy had nine children, eight of whom are pictured here. John Kennedy stands third from the right, alongside his parents.

once played a game of "chicken" on their bikes, riding them at full speed toward the other to see who would turn away first. They collided head-on. Joe was unhurt, John's injuries required 28 stitches.

Like his older brother, John Kennedy in 1936 attended Harvard University. In 1937, President Franklin Roosevelt appointed Joseph Kennedy Sr. ambassador to Great Britain, a prestigious and important role.

For John, his famous family became a part of life to deal with, and he did so with dignity. During college, he would occasionally see plays in which the Kennedys were the subject of jokes. John laughed along with the audiences. Despite being somebody raised with riches, Kennedy was not aloof or unkind.

As he matured, he became somebody who working people liked, admired, and trusted. He learned compassion early in life.

His younger sister, Rosemary, was born with mental disabilities. In those times, it was common to send such children to institutions, but Joseph and Rosemary Kennedy tried for years to keep her at home. They also insisted that Rosemary's brothers and sisters treat her as an equal, which they all did.

Not many saw John Kennedy's compassion first-hand. But a lot of Americans would read about his courage. Kennedy entered the U.S. Navy in October of 1941, just a few months before the United States was plunged into World War II. Despite severe health problems that included a constantly painful back, Kennedy asked for active duty instead of the office jobs he was first given. He was put in charge of a PT (patrol-torpedo) boat. It was one of the most dangerous jobs in military service. When his father arranged to have him made a trainer instead of a fighter, John Kennedy was furious. He argued with the military officials until they agreed to let him go into combat zones.

Kennedy's bravery showed itself during the war. His boat, PT-109, was rammed and split in half by a Japanese destroyer. Kennedy and the survivors of the crash were sent into the ocean. He and five other members first clung to the hull of the boat. Kennedy and two others swam out and helped five more crew members back to the floating wreckage. Two men died and were never found.

After nine hours of holding onto the boat, Kennedy and the other survivors made their way to a small island in the distance. Swimming on his stomach, Kennedy towed one of his injured crewmen by clenching the lifejacket ties in his teeth while the crewman floated behind. It was a five-hour swim. Once they made

Kennedy receives a medal for his service during his Navy years.

it to the island, Kennedy decided to swim out and flag down a boat. Most had believed the crew died in the sinking of PT-109. After seven days, ravaged by thirst and hunger, the survivors were rescued. The dramatic story of PT-109 and Kennedy's care for his men raised spirits back home. It was exactly the kind of story Americans needed to hear in wartime.

Kennedy's status as an American hero played well after the war. Two years into peacetime, he entered politics and ran for the U.S. House of Representatives. He hadn't always been interested in politics. His family, in fact, had been counting on his older brother, Joe, to run for office. Strong, outgoing, and handsome, Joe Kennedy seemed destined to be a politician after his military service. During World War II, he flew bombers over Europe and completed 25 successful missions. But during a high-risk mission on August 12, 1944, his plane exploded. Joe Kennedy and another pilot were killed. John Kennedy had lost his older brother and role model.

After the war Kennedy was looking at two career choices — law and journalism. Neither possibility thrilled him. He saw being a lawyer as too boring compared to actually making laws to help the country. He saw journalism as being too much an observer, not a participant, in important events.

He saw in politics, however, an opportunity to make a difference, to strengthen and defend his country. Helped in large part by his father's money, Kennedy entered the Congressional race in Massachusetts at age 29. He easily won a seat in the House of Representatives in 1946.

Kennedy served three terms before running for and winning a seat in the U.S. Senate. In his run for Senate, he brought in his younger brother Robert to run the campaign. Robert, known as "Bobby," was working as a lawyer for the U.S. Department of Justice.

John F. Kennedy and his wife, Jacqueline, during the 1960 presidential campaign

In 1953, about a year after he was elected to the Senate, Kennedy married Jacqueline Bouvier. The two had met in 1951 at a dinner party. They had a lot in common. Most obviously, both were young, attractive members of wealthy families.

In the time Kennedy was in Congress, lawmakers were greatly concerned about communism and Soviet Russia's intent on world domination. He would deal with those issues more than once during his presidency.

As his time in Congress went on, Kennedy's ambition grew. His six years in the Senate saw him emerge as a leader on foreign affairs. He had proven himself an expert on foreign policy, and he did so as a fresh young voice in a government run mostly by old men. As early as 1956, when he sought unsuccessfully to be the vice-presidential nominee for the Democrats, his name was mentioned as a promising candidate for president. Kennedy felt he could do more as president than as senator, and he announced in January 1960 that he would run.

Kennedy and Lyndon B. Johnson campaign in Austin, Texas.

John F. Kennedy (left) and Richard Nixon (right) during a 1960 televised presidential debate

The election pitted him against Republican Richard Nixon. In some ways, it was a battle of styles. Television was replacing radio as a source for news, and Kennedy's youth, good looks, and comfort on TV gave him an advantage. Nixon often looked nervous and uncomfortable on TV. (Their debates have been used as examples of how important it became to look good on television.) But Nixon had been vice president under Dwight Eisenhower, and earlier he had served with distinction in noncombat roles during World War II.

The election race was close and hard-fought. Winning by the slightest margin, John F. Kennedy became 35th president of the United States. He was the youngest man ever elected to the office. He also represented the hopes and dreams of an entire country.

Lee Harvey Oswald

CHAPTER 2
THE MAKING OF A KILLER

Lee Harvey Oswald moved through life confused and angry. He saw himself as a world-class soldier, a great thinker, and a political expert. Reality kept showing otherwise. His high opinion of himself was simply not shared by many.

By the time he cleared a spot on the sixth floor of the brick building where he worked in Dallas and pointed his rifle at the back of John F. Kennedy's head, he was not doing well in life. He was, in fact, a near-broke father of two children with a crumbling marriage and low-paying job that involved moving cardboard boxes of textbooks.

Likely, Oswald did what he did because, like other assassins before and after him, he had a twisted desire to be as famous as the person he killed. He achieved world fame, but as nothing but a killer who denied the world a popular, effective leader.

If Oswald had some political reason to murder his president —

any reason — he took it to the grave. He never spoke of hating or even disliking the president, and he loved to speak his mind. As a teen Oswald spoke of disliking then-president Dwight D. Eisenhower, but as an adult Oswald rarely if ever spoke ill of John F. Kennedy. At the time he shot Kennedy, Oswald's political passions were in support of Communist-controlled Cuba, the island country that caused President Kennedy so much grief.

Oswald was born into a troubled family. His father died a few months before Lee's birth in New Orleans, Louisiana, in 1939. Oswald had a childhood swamped by change after change. His mother struggled to find good work and pay the bills. Much of Oswald's early childhood was spent either with an aunt or, once he was 3 years old, with his brothers at a home for orphans and children with one parent. It was called the Bethlehem Children's Home.

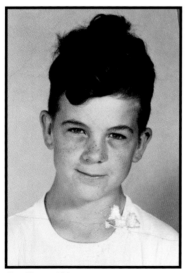

Oswald as a child

After his mother married again in the 1940s, Lee's older brothers attended military school. But Lee stayed home and found himself watching an increasingly unhappy marriage. His mother and stepfather fought frequently and eventually divorced.

His difficult family life continued as he moved from city to city while his mother pursued work. By the time Lee moved to Fort Worth, Texas, the family had moved 16 times. Still, Lee at first did well in most subjects at school. He attended classes quietly and paid attention. But by age 13, living in New York with his mother, he began having problems. Skipping school was one of them. A Youth Court judge placed him in a home for boys, where one social worker saw him as seriously withdrawn and troubled.

The social worker wrote of him: "It seems fairly clear that he has detached himself from the world around him because no one in it ever met any of his needs for love."

As a high school student in the 1950s, Oswald became fascinated with communism, a system of government at odds with American ideals of freedom. Communism was growing among eastern European nations, in Southeast Asia, and elsewhere. Its leaders sought world control, clearly seen as a threat to the way of life in the United States.

The world had entered a period called the Cold War. That was the term applied to years of tension between the United States and the Soviet Union (and other communist-controlled or communist-leaning countries) after World War II. Oswald would go on to embrace communism at a time when the U.S. population — including U.S. Senator John F. Kennedy — grew increasingly nervous about its spread. American communists, in fact, were required to register with the government.

Driving Oswald's deep attraction to communism may have been its principle that the workers of the world were being pushed around by the rich and powerful. Oswald likely felt he had been pushed around too much, by everybody from the Youth Court judge to kids who liked to beat him up. It's also possible that, given his family situation and his inability to make friends, he simply sought a group to which he could belong.

Oswald dropped out of high school and at age 17 enlisted in the U.S. Marines, serving for three years in both the United States and Japan. He showed more problem behavior in the Marines. First he accidentally shot himself with an unregistered handgun. Later he assaulted a superior officer. That led to his serving 45 days in military jail.

Oswald during his Marines stint

While in the Marines, he read books on Marxism and communism and dreamed of someday moving to Russia. Oswald finally faked a hardship case to get an early discharge. He claimed he had to take care of his mother. Soon after he was released, however, he traveled to Moscow, the capital of the Soviet Union and the power center of communism. Once there, he took steps to become a Soviet citizen, but he was denied. Oswald went so far as visiting the U.S. Embassy in Moscow to renounce his American citizenship. He even attempted suicide rather than return to the U.S.

His devotion to communism, however, wasn't very sophisticated. An American Embassy official asked him not only about why he wanted to stay in the Soviet Union but about communism itself. Oswald, it turned out, didn't know all that much about it. That official later said Oswald had a "flaky" enthusiasm and "didn't have the slightest idea what this country (the Soviet Union) was all about."

In the meeting at the embassy, Oswald made a vague threat. He said he could offer the Soviets information he had as the result of his time in the Marines. The American official quickly notified the U.S. government about what Oswald said. He also told the Moscow chief of United Press International news service to seek Oswald out for a news story.

Oswald agreed to be interviewed by an American journalist. In early November 1959, American newspapers including the *New York Times* carried the bizarre story of the American Marine who wanted to become a Soviet citizen. So, for a while, Oswald was getting attention and recognition. He defended his anti-American views in a letter to his brother, writing at one point: "In the event of war I would kill any American who put a uniform on in defense of the American government — any American."

While keeping him under close watch in case he was an American spy, the Soviets allowed Oswald to stay in the country for at least a year. They assigned him a factory job in a town 400 miles from Moscow. Once he got a full taste of Russian work life, though, Oswald began to have second thoughts. As he wrote in a diary (his spelling corrected here), "I am starting to reconsider my desire about staying. The work is drab, the money I get has nowhere to be spent. No nightclubs or bowling alleys, no places of recreation except the trade union dances. I have had enough."

He was also shocked to discover the Soviet system was nothing like the ideal society he thought it would be. Just like the American economy, communism had its share of rich people and poor people. It was not a system where everyone was treated equally and fairly. In February 1961 he began asking for his American passport back and stated his desire to return to the United States.

While he awaited an answer, Oswald fell in love with a Russian woman, Marina Prusakova. The two met at a dance. They married in April 1961, later having a daughter, whom they named June. Oswald received permission to return to the U.S. In June 1962, the family left Russia and arrived in Fort Worth, Texas, where Oswald's brother and mother lived. Oswald's first words to his brother upon getting off the plane were: "No reporters?"

The two lived with Oswald's family for a while, and in the summer of 1962, Oswald found work at a welding company. In the fall, however, he told Marina and friends he had been fired and needed to move to Dallas to find more work. There he found a job in a printing house and rented a small, dirty apartment for his family.

Oswald was at that time subscribing to Communist newspapers and magazines. At one point, he sought to join the Socialist Workers Party.

On March 12, 1963, Oswald used a fake name to purchase two guns by mail — a handgun and a World War II model Italian rifle with a scope. Both guns would be used on November 22, 1963.

Oswald asked his wife to photograph him as he posed with his guns.

He told Marina they were for hunting someday. She was mad he bothered with this expense when the family was low on food.

By this time, Oswald was writing a journal that indicated he was upset with the Communist Party of the United States as well as the Soviets. In his writings, he called for a new party that would "bring about the final destruction" of American society.

Lee Oswald with his wife, Marina, and their infant daughter in Russia in 1962

The communist revolt in Cuba captured Oswald's attention. In March 1963, he began writing to a group called Fair Play for Cuba Committee, which was critical of Kennedy's treatment of Cuba. Oswald stood on a busy street corner in Dallas and passed out pro-Cuba pamphlets. The materials criticized the U.S. for not welcoming Cuba's move toward communism under its new leader, Fidel Castro.

Oswald had other plans to draw attention to himself. He asked his wife to take a photo of him holding his new rifle in one hand and two Marxist newspapers, *The Worker* and *The Militant*, in the other. This photo also shows him holstering a pistol. He told his wife he was going to send the photo to *The Militant* to show he was "ready for anything."

Oswald did just that. He sent the photo to *The Militant.* The woman who handled the newspaper's subscriptions saw the picture of a "kooky" looking guy holding a gun and the two papers. She thought it quite odd that the two newspapers represented opposite viewpoints on political matters. The entire point of the photo, she thought, was "really dumb and totally naive."

A few weeks after the guns arrived in the mail, Oswald lost his job at the printing company. At some point, Oswald's view of himself switched to something far more sinister than a socialist. He saw himself as an assassin, and his first target was a former U.S. Army general named Edwin Walker.

Walker was a leader in the John Birch Society, a national group formed in 1958. The group was considered ultra-conservative and anti-communist. Walker was a champion to those who feared both communism and equal rights for African Americans. Walker had become a controversial figure and had even defended the likes of George Lincoln Rockwell, head of the American Nazi Party.

Walker's return to Dallas had taken place on the same day Oswald told his family he needed to find work in that city. Oswald spent weeks watching Walker's home and taking photos. Then on April 10, 1963, he stood outside the home with a gun. Oswald spotted Walker through a window, aimed, and fired. Oswald fled immediately, stashing the gun at the scene.

He discovered by reading the newspapers the following day that his shot missed. Walker had survived the attack. Nobody traced the shooting to Oswald, not even when he returned to the scene the following day to retrieve the rifle.

Oswald distributing pro-Cuba flyers in New Orleans, Louisiana, in August 1963

Oswald soon moved with his wife and child to New Orleans. He made a minor name for himself again by handing out pro-Cuba materials on the streets and being interviewed on the radio about his support for the communists there. He took a job at a coffee company in New Orleans. At work he behaved like a loner and paid little attention to his duties. His wife was pregnant again and, at times, was afraid of Oswald's violent temper. She left him in New Orleans and moved to a Dallas suburb. Oswald attempted to get permission to visit Cuba, saying he would continue traveling to the Soviet Union. But neither country seemed eager to have him and denied his immediate requests.

Lee Harvey Oswald returned to Dallas in October 1963. He was living in a rented room and trying to reconcile with his wife. Marina, who would soon give birth to their second daughter, told him about a possible job. Marina said she had met a woman whose brother just found a job and could maybe help Oswald get one at the same place. Connections were made, and on October 16, 1963, Oswald began working at the Texas School Book Depository. Little more than a month later, he would aim his rifle through an open window on the building's sixth floor. He would kill the president from there.

Communist leaders Fidel Castro (left) of Cuba and Nikita Khrushchev of the Soviet Union

CHAPTER 3
A TIME OF DANGER

In his time as president, John F. Kennedy handled some of the most dangerous threats ever posed to the United States. Many historians now consider it safe to say he was the right leader at the right time. His leadership protected freedom and might have prevented nuclear war.

If things had gone wrong, we might not be here, comfortably reading about that point in history. Thousands if not millions of people might have died from nuclear strikes in a fight to the death with the Soviet Union. The environment Kennedy inherited as president was dangerously tense between the communists in Soviet Russia and the United States.

That tension and struggle, called the Cold War, began after World War II. The U.S., Great Britain, and the Soviet Union had been allies in defeating Hitler's Germany. But the allies did not agree on what should happen after their victory. The Soviets began installing and supporting communist governments in eastern Europe. Communism took hold in countries such as Poland, Hungary, Romania, and Czechoslovakia.

Communism put the government's needs before people. It kept tight control over everything from a country's economy to religion to freedom to live wherever one chose. This went against American ideals of democracy and freedom, and the spread of communism to any country, near or far, was seen as a threat and something to be fought against and wiped out wherever possible.

Making matters more hostile was the development of nuclear weapons. Both the United States and the Soviet Union now had nuclear weapons — aimed at each other.

In 1961, Kennedy took charge of a plan started under the previous president. In 1959 the pro-U.S. government of Cuba had been overthrown by rebels loyal to Fidel Castro, who became Cuba's president. Castro's ties with the Soviet Union made the U.S. military and political leaders nervous. In response, the U.S. secretly trained more than 1,400 Cubans to invade the country. The hope was that the invasion would inspire other Cubans to overtake and kick out Castro and his Soviet-supported government.

President Kennedy's advisers from the military and the Central Intelligence Agency (CIA) told him it would go smoothly. They said the invasion would appear to be a Cuban uprising, nothing involving the United States. Kennedy hesitantly approved the plan. The invaders would use disguised U.S. planes and ships to launch their invasion at Cuba's Bay of Pigs.

The operation failed at every end. Paratroopers landed in the wrong places. Ships sank before hitting the shore. In the

Captured U.S.-backed soldiers after the failed Bay of Pigs invasion

end, more than 100 of the invaders were killed, and more than 1,200 surrendered. Some advisers pressured Kennedy to send U.S. troops into the mess, but he refused. The president was furious and blamed the CIA and the military advisers — the Joint Chiefs of Staff — for misleading him about the plan.

From that point on, the president would always weigh the opinion of military leaders with some distrust. Eventually his guarded attitude about the opinions of military advisers served him well. It might've been what prevented the U.S. and the Soviet Union from bombing each other with nuclear weapons.

The Bay of Pigs certainly did not ease the relationship between the U.S. and Soviet Union. The head of the Soviet government, Nikita Khrushchev, continually boasted that communism was the superior form of government. He also accused the U.S. of wanting to start military conflicts.

The failure in Cuba weakened Kennedy's approach when it came to a showdown with the Soviets over Berlin. After World War II, Germany had been split into four zones, each controlled by one of the four Allied powers who defeated the Germans: the U.S., France, Great Britain, and the Soviet Union. Although Berlin was in the Soviets' occupation zone and under Communist control, it was also divided between east and west. The United States, France, and Britain controlled West Berlin, and the Soviets occupied East Berlin.

But Khrushchev called for an end to that deal in 1958. He insisted that the U.S., Britain, and France get out of Berlin so the Soviets could unite the city. The Soviet system had not been

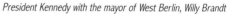
President Kennedy with the mayor of West Berlin, Willy Brandt

working well in East Berlin. More and more people were crossing over into West Berlin, embarrassing the Soviets and ruining their hopes of a strong Communist city. The U.S. refused to move out, protecting freedom in West Berlin.

This was the situation when Kennedy took office, and meetings between the old Communist Khrushchev and the young U.S. president did not go well. Khrushchev, loud and colorful but often insulting, had the upper hand in conversations. The stakes were high, and Kennedy was under frequent pressure to consider a war plan to save West Berlin. After the two met in Vienna, Khrushchev made matters worse by halting progress toward a ban on nuclear weapons testing.

In a televised address, Kennedy explained the situation to the American people. He told them that he wasn't going to let the Soviets take over West Berlin. He said, "We cannot and will not permit the communists to drive us out of Berlin, either gradually or by force . . . we will at all times be ready to talk, if talk will help. But we must also be ready to resist with force, if force is used upon us."

With both sides firm, the world watched to see who would make the next move. Less than a month after Kennedy's get-tough speech, East German forces threw up barriers that blocked access from East Berlin to West Berlin, eventually constructing a wall.

Realizing the U.S. would not back down, Khrushchev had decided upon this solution. It struck Kennedy that Khrushchev was no longer interested in taking over West Berlin. "This is his way out of a predicament," Kennedy said. "It's not a very nice solution, but a wall is a hell of a lot better than a war."

Compared to the Bay of Pigs, this was a win. After the wall was built, Kennedy helped cool a showdown between tanks aiming at each other from opposite sides of the wall. Talking directly to Khrushchev, Kennedy offered that if the Soviet Union pulled its tanks, the U.S. would as well.

Not a year later, the distrust between the U.S. and the Soviet Union boiled up again. Tensions led to what is known as the Cuban Missile Crisis — considered by some to be Kennedy's shining moment (or shining days) in the White House.

Because Khrushchev was worried that the U.S. was planning to overthrow Cuba, he decided to use Cuba as a nuclear missile base. In October 1962, Khrushchev began shipping missiles to Cuba, an island about 90 miles from Florida. The Soviets sent missiles that could carry nuclear weapons 1,000 miles into the U.S. They sent other missiles that could travel 2,000 miles.

It was Cold War thinking: The U.S. had missiles in Turkey and Italy, both near Soviet-controlled territory. So Khrushchev believed he should give Americans a taste of what it was like having nuclear weapons pointed at them from a short distance away. Kennedy wanted no such taste. He was determined to not let shipments of those missiles get through to the island country so near to the U.S.

But Soviet ships were heading for Cuba with parts to keep building missiles. The Soviets were deliberately provoking the U.S. to either act or stand by while nuclear weapons were assembled. Kennedy needed to figure out how to stop the shipments and the buildup in Cuba without sparking war.

To invade Cuba, as his military advisers pressed him to do,

A U.S. destroyer (at front) and Navy plane escort a Soviet freighter carrying missiles away from Cuba.

would be an act of war. Such an act surely could trigger a nuclear exchange with the Soviets. Kennedy sought advice for any possible peaceful way out, all while the Soviets insisted on their right to build the missiles for their own protection.

Kennedy decided an invasion had to be a last resort. He put U.S. Navy ships around Cuba to prevent Soviet ships from reaching it. If the move failed, air strikes and an invasion of Cuba would follow — as would a probable nuclear strike. Congressional leaders insisted that the blockade was a sign of weakness. They urged Kennedy to strike Cuba quickly.

On a Monday night, Americans heard from their president that Cuba was installing nuclear weapons and the missiles could hit Washington, D.C., or any other city in the American southeast. Kennedy said the U.S. could not tolerate this advance and would "quarantine" Cuba. The U.S. was blocking all offensive weapons from reaching the island. If the Soviet didn't stop the buildup, the U.S. would take action, Kennedy explained. If Cuba used any of the nuclear missiles already in place against the U.S., the U.S. would use nuclear missiles against the Soviet Union.

On October 25, 1962, a few Soviet ships began turning around. They were followed by more. Kennedy had once again kept his more aggressive advisers at bay while he tried to reason with Khrushchev. In what seemed the last minute, Khrushchev agreed to turn the missiles around and eliminate them from Cuba. In return, he was promised the U.S. would leave Cuba alone. As he had with Berlin, Kennedy found a way to not be persuaded by those who were itching for war.

Biographer Robert Dallek writes that Kennedy's greatest achievements as president "were his management of Soviet-American relations and his effectiveness in discouraging a U.S. military mindset that accepted the possibility — indeed, even likelihood — of a nuclear war with Moscow."

The world did not get to benefit from Kennedy's calm and thoughtful approach when it came to what would become America's longest war up to that point: the war in Vietnam. In this distant Asian country, communist-led North Vietnam was fighting against South Vietnam, which was backed by the United States. If South Vietnam fell to the communists, it was feared, neighboring countries would follow what was called a "domino effect."

Kennedy was familiar with the struggles in Vietnam, which

until the 1950s had been under the control of France. He was uncertain about how the U.S. should respond to the push southward by the North Vietnamese. Again, his top aides all believed military action was a good idea. Secretary of State Dean Rusk and Defense Secretary Robert McNamara reported that the fall of South Vietnam would be "extremely dangerous."

By late 1963 South Vietnamese forces had been joined by 16,000 American military "advisers." The U.S. troops were there to advise and guide the South Vietnamese army. But the situation grew worse every day. The North Vietnamese kept striking. Reporters on the scene were doing stories that opposed the optimistic reports made by the Kennedy advisers.

South Vietnamese President Ngo Diem was losing the support of his people. Finally, Kennedy authorized a military removal of Diem, which resulted in Diem being assassinated. This was not the result Kennedy expected. He increasingly realized how chaotic this conflict could be, and he knew it needed to be addressed somehow.

Nearly every member of his national security and defense team called for U.S. troops to fight on behalf of South Vietnam before the country fell to communism. Kennedy's experience told him he needn't take his advisers' word as the final say. He believed communism was a threat to world security. But he also saw that this country was more than 8,000 miles away and that the South's army of 200,000 was not having any success. Was it worth sending young Americans to fight and die?

Kennedy had a lot to think about when his plane landed in Dallas in November 1963.

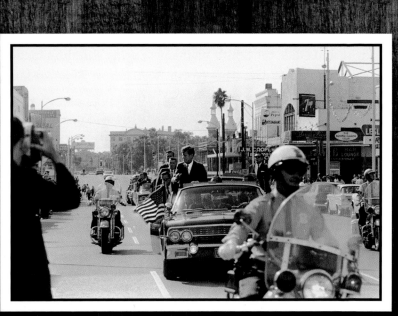

President Kennedy visited Tampa, Florida, before traveling to Texas in November 1963.

CHAPTER 4
A SHOCKING CRIME

In the early autumn of 1963, Kennedy had not said publicly that he would run for re-election the following year. But it seemed he was already campaigning. In September, the president visited nine states in less than one week. Although the visits were supposed to be about preserving natural resources, the speeches carried the feel of campaign stops. His talks eventually covered more exciting areas of concern such as world peace, education, and national security.

By November 1963, a year before the 1964 presidential election, Kennedy had begun serious campaign planning. His chances of winning were good. By the end of 1962, he was listed as the world leader admired most by Americans. In March 1963, polling showed most Americans believed he would be elected for a second term.

But he didn't want to take chances, and he knew he wasn't popular in at least two Southern states, Florida and Texas. He visited Florida on November 18, speaking to large groups in Tampa and Miami about the economy and foreign affairs.

On November 21 the president and his wife began what was to be a two-day, five-city tour of Texas. As far as Kennedy could tell, the Democratic party in Texas needed some repair. Opposing groups within the party were fighting each other — in some cases literally coming to blows. Kennedy believed a visit to the state could get Texas voters behind him and his Texan vice president, Lyndon Johnson. The rift in the party was especially strong in Dallas, so Kennedy made sure he would visit the city.

On the morning of November 22, Kennedy woke in Fort Worth. He soon spoke to a gathering of residents on the need for America's leadership in defense, space, and economic freedom. He later addressed the Fort Worth Chamber of Commerce. From that city, Kennedy took a 13-minute flight to Dallas, where he and Jackie were greeted by a cheering crowd offering their hands and a bouquet of red roses for Jackie. After shaking hands and talking with the crowd, the First Couple took the back seat of a convertible that would carry them on a parade through the streets of Dallas. In the seat in front of them were Texas Governor John Connally and his wife, Nellie.

A lunch speech by the president had been scheduled, and the president had agreed that they would drive through downtown Dallas. The drive would allow the president to wave from the back seat of the convertible to the hundreds of people gathered along the streets to catch a glimpse of him.

A few days earlier *The Dallas Morning News* had published a report on the route. The motorcade would travel first through

The Kennedys arrive at the Dallas airport shortly before the president's assassination.

downtown Dallas. The last segment would be a stretch in Dealey Plaza, a three-acre patch of grass and office buildings known as the "Front Door of Dallas." From there, the car would speed up and take the freeway to the president's destination, the Trade Mart, where he was scheduled to address an audience of about 2,000 people.

When the car turned onto Elm Street, it would pass below the Texas School Book Depository. Lee Harvey Oswald would be watching from above, rifle at his side.

The presidential motorcade in downtown Dallas before it proceeded to Dealey Plaza

The Kennedys rode in a convertible with the governor of Texas, John Connally, and his wife, Nellie.

That morning Oswald had been given a ride to work by a friend, who asked about the long bag Oswald was carrying. Oswald explained that it held curtain rods. Using the freight elevator or the stairs, Oswald arrived on the sixth floor of the building, stashed his rifle nearby and began working — filling boxes with books.

For the next three hours, Oswald appeared to be just doing what he was supposed to do. Lunch hour approached, and while hundreds of people had crowded the downtown route, the Dealey Plaza section of the route — the final stretch — held fewer people. This was the stretch where the motorcade would finish up its slow, parade-like pace. Some people along the route were a mere six or seven feet from the president himself.

Oswald, finding himself alone on the sixth floor, eventually took his rifle and waited at a window for the moment he knew would come. When the motorcade turned on Elm Street and began traveling away from the building, Oswald aimed at the back of the president and began firing.

He fired three shots in a matter of seconds. The first shot missed, and the sound was mistaken by some in the president's motorcade as a motorcycle backfiring. Three and a half seconds later, the second shot was fired. This one hit Kennedy in the back. Connally too, was hit by the bullet and shouted, "They're going to kill us all." Connally's wife, Nellie, pulled him close to her, resting his head on her lap as she tried to protect him from the unknown line of fire.

Jackie Kennedy turned to the wounded president as the shots rang out.

Confused, Jackie Kennedy looked at her husband and the odd look on his face, as though he was suffering a headache. Just as the Secret Service called for the motorcade to speed up and head toward the hospital, a third shot pierced the back of the president's skull, tearing open his head. His body slumped and leaned into Jackie, who was now covered with her husband's blood.

The motorcade raced to Parkland Hospital, as news reports began explaining that the president had been shot, perhaps fatally. The situation was dire. While emergency room surgeons worked to save Governor Connally's life, the doctors were helpless against the terrible wounds Kennedy had suffered. Efforts to save him failed. The president was pronounced dead at 1 p.m.

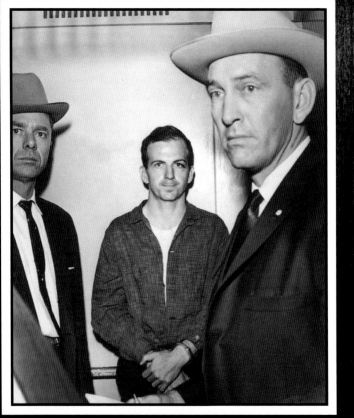

Lee Harvey Oswald in the custody of police after the assassination.

CHAPTER 5
THE TROUBLING AFTERMATH

After firing three times, Lee Harvey Oswald dashed toward the back staircase. He hid the rifle between some boxes and ran down the stairway. On the way down, he encountered a police officer who was heading upstairs along with the Book Depository's manager. The two talked to Oswald briefly, with the manager explaining that Oswald belonged in the building as an employee. The officer continued up the stairs, and Oswald slipped into the pandemonium and confusion that overwhelmed the streets.

Oswald calmly walked seven blocks along Elm Street. He flagged down a city bus and, despite not being at a bus stop, the driver let him board. The bus had to slow down considerably because of the jammed traffic and panic in the area. Oswald got off the bus and hailed a taxi to take him to his rooming house, where he changed clothes, grabbed his pistol, and walked out.

Soon a Dallas police officer named J.D. Tippit noticed a man who sort of fit the physical description of the suspect given to police by witnesses. Tippit radioed for more specific descriptions while following the walking man slowly. Eventually Tippit pulled his squad car to the curb so he could ask the man, Oswald, some questions. Oswald approached the car and, through the open passenger window, talked with Tippit. When the officer got out of the car to talk further, Oswald pulled out his pistol and fired four shots at Tippit, killing him.

Then Oswald fled a few blocks, and as sirens wailed in response to the killing of Tippit, he ducked into a movie theater, sitting among the back rows. He wasn't there for long. Ten minutes later the lights in the theater glared on and police entered, capturing and arresting Oswald on suspicion of murdering Officer Tippit.

Police, meanwhile, had also found the rifle Oswald stashed in the book depository, as well as his bag and the empty shells. They would soon discover through serial number research that it was the gun purchased by Oswald through the mail. They found the same was true of the pistol used to kill officer Tippit.

The world watched Oswald as Dallas police allowed reporters to question him. He insisted he was innocent. He said upon being arrested that he wasn't sure what he was being charged with and denied any wrongdoing. Through reporters, Oswald asked for lawyers to step forward and help him, claiming he was "just a patsy."

"I didn't shoot anybody," he said at one point. "I haven't been told what I am here for." He also claimed that he was being held because he had lived in the Soviet Union.

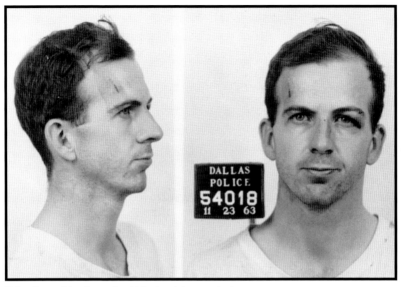

Police photos of Lee Harvey Oswald the day of the assassination

On November 24, Americans watched their television sets to see the memorial service for President Kennedy. Also that day Dallas police were moving Oswald from police headquarters to another location. The police had invited the press to film the transport, and as one network broadcast live on television, a man in a dark suit and hat moved forward, shoved a pistol at Oswald, and fired into his stomach. Oswald fell. The shooter, a nightclub owner named Jack Ruby, was arrested. Oswald was taken by ambulance to the same hospital where Kennedy had been taken.

Oswald died less than two hours after being shot, making no admission in the meantime of having done anything wrong. Investigations into his life and background found no clear reason why Oswald decided to assassinate Kennedy. Some people believe

Jack Ruby emerged from the crowd and shot Oswald as officers escorted him through the lower level of the Dallas police station.

he wanted to prove himself to Soviet leaders as devoted to the Soviet cause. Whatever his motives were, they remain foggy even today.

The United States had lost a beloved president, and the free world lost a skilled leader. The question of why John Kennedy was killed would prove to be a difficult one to answer. Many people thought Oswald was part of a larger plan rather than one troubled man acting alone. But careful and thorough investigations have concluded that Oswald was alone in plotting and carrying out his crime.

With time, people began to wonder how the United States and the world might be different today had John Kennedy survived. Lyndon Johnson, who was sworn in as president soon after Kennedy's death, led the country in trying times. Historians now praise Johnson's work to promote civil rights and to assure fairness for African Americans and other minorities. But under Johnson, the country would plunge itself into war in Vietnam. The war and his handling of it cast a dark shadow over Johnson's presidency.

Ho Chi Minh, leader of the Vietnamese communist revolutionaries

History presents an important question here. How would Kennedy have handled the Vietnam War had he lived? Might many lives have been saved? Might years of political unrest and division have been avoided?

These are painful questions, because 58,000 American lives and 2 million Vietnamese lives were lost in the war. And in the end, many people say the war changed nothing.

By the time he was shot, Kennedy in his 1,000 days in office had earned a reputation as a true world leader, tough and thoughtful. He gained that reputation in the most difficult ways imaginable. More than once he made decisions that, if wrong, would have cost thousands of lives, perhaps millions.

So how would he have handled our country's approach to Vietnam? During the few early years of the conflict, Kennedy did deal with it. His choices and thoughts in those years give a good idea of how to answer the question.

In the 1950s and early 1960s, not many Americans had heard of Vietnam, located more than 8,000 miles away in Southeast Asia. Until 1954 Vietnam and neighboring Laos and Cambodia had been under the control of France in what was called French Indochina.

That ended in 1954 when communist rebels led by Ho Chi Minh staged a four-month attack. They overpowered the French in the city of Dien Bien Phu in the northern part of Vietnam. The country was split into two nations, the communist-controlled North Vietnam and the independent, pro-U.S. country of South Vietnam.

Army units from North Vietnam, however, continued pressing into South Vietnam. Soldiers and leaders from the North saw their fight as one for Vietnamese independence. The U.S. perceived it as — or mistook it for — the spread of communism directed from China and Russia. From former president Dwight Eisenhower on down, officials had been terrified of more communist countries in the world. If South Vietnam fell, it was feared, the communists would control all of Southeast Asia. Before he left office, President Eisenhower sent military support and about 700 non-combat military personnel to Vietnam to help and train its army.

Fresh into his presidency in 1961, Kennedy had looked carefully at the Vietnam situation with one main goal — keeping American soldiers out of the conflict. He agreed to help South Vietnamese President Ngo Dinh Diem by giving him money to expand the South Vietnamese army to a total of 200,000 people.

U.S. helicopters airlifted Vietnamese soldiers into battle against communist forces in 1965.

Diem's government proved to be nothing but a headache to the United States. He behaved like a power-hungry tyrant — the worst possible example of democracy. Aside from his personal greed, he abused his own people. He violently suppressed the rights of the country's Buddhists, who were the country's majority. While supporting Diem with money and equipment, Kennedy urged Diem to change course. He told Diem that democracy in South Vietnam wasn't going to work out so well if most of its people detested him.

Diem constantly called for American help, knowing the U.S. was committed to keeping communism from spreading. In 1961 Kennedy again found himself one of the few people in his circle of advisers against going to war. His advisers told him the U.S. should send between 22,800 and 40,000 soldiers and take over the war from Diem.

Kennedy had not liked the idea of such an open-ended conflict. How could battles in distant jungles end well for the U.S.? In October 1961 he sent military officials and other advisers to visit Vietnam. He expected them to come back with the best possible plan. They returned with bad news: The U.S. couldn't act soon enough to prevent South Vietnam's fall to the communists. His advisers presented a plan calling for a "limited partnership" with the South Vietnamese in which 8,000 American troops would be sent to fight. Others who made the visit, including Kennedy's defense secretary, Robert McNamara, suggested sending 200,000 American soldiers.

While he and others knew South Vietnam could be lost to the Communists, Kennedy remained unconvinced about a military response. He questioned the idea of getting America involved in fighting in another country's civil war. What he told a newspaper reporter in 1961 turned out to be eerily accurate. Sending thousands of fighting troops would likely lead to demands for even more.

"They want a force of American troops," Kennedy said. "They say it's necessary in order to restore confidence and maintain morale. But . . . the troops will march in; the bands will play; the crowds will cheer; and in four days everyone will have forgotten. Then we will be told we have to send in more troops. It's like taking a drink. The effect wears off, and you have to take another."

During an interview with Walter Cronkite of CBS News, President Kennedy had expressed doubts about South Vietnam's ability to win the war and questioned the actions of President Ngo Dinh Diem.

Kennedy decided to provide more equipment and to more than double the 1,200 non-combat military advisers already there.

That term, "military advisers," had been an important one. It allowed Kennedy to help South Vietnam with American soldiers who could aid in battling the North Vietnamese but could not enter direct combat. It was a thin line, where helping ended and fighting began. Some people accused Kennedy of not being honest with the American people about military activity in the country.

He defended himself at a press conference, saying, "We have not sent combat troops in the generally understood sense of the word."

Kennedy continued to send these advisers — up to 16,000 by October 1963 — to help Diem. These advisers were no doubt seeing combat action in their aid of the South Vietnamese. More than a hundred American advisers were killed by the end of the year.

In 1963, Kennedy had been growing increasingly upset with Diem, whose rule was so corrupt and oppressive that it made communism a lot more attractive to the South Vietnamese. Diem had outlawed all political parties but his own and cracked down on any protests of his government. He even allowed for the killing of Buddhists who were peacefully demonstrating.

Kennedy had finally approved a secret plan for the military in South Vietnam to overthrow Diem. On November 2, 1963, Diem and his brother — a top adviser — were not only removed from office but assassinated. The result was chaos, and the North Vietnamese grew bolder. The U.S. now found itself further tangled up in a situation that troubled its leaders. At least some American leaders doubted the war was winnable.

Kennedy may have had enough. Even before Diem's overthrow, Kennedy announced his desire to bring 1,000 troops home by the year's end. With advisers he had discussed the goal of having all American troops out by 1965.

Shortly before leaving for Dallas in November, Kennedy told Mike Forrestal, his advisor on Far East Affairs, to put together every option available in Vietnam, "including how we get out of there."

Would Kennedy have removed the U.S. from Vietnam by 1965? Some actions he took in Vietnam give us clues. It's also important to look at the amount of caution Kennedy demonstrated not only in Vietnam, but throughout his presidency. His firm but careful responses had led to relatively peaceful results in conflicts with the Soviets. Of course, we can't know what Kennedy would have done about Vietnam. Many historians today believe he would have continued to back the South Vietnamese, just as his successor did.

In 1965, under Lyndon B. Johnson, the

President Lyndon B. Johnson

U.S. entered the war in Vietnam. Over the next 10 years, the war would cost many lives and tear apart those who supported the war and those who did not. And in the end, the North Vietnamese overtook South Vietnam.

Johnson faced an overwhelming push from every angle — military advisers, the media, and the public — to go into Vietnam and stop the spread of communism. Kennedy would have faced that as well. But Kennedy had something Johnson did not. He had experience dealing with military men who saw combat and war as a first option. Kennedy had a distrust for military leaders. It went back to his time in the Navy, and as president he'd watched top level military men talk seriously of nuclear war. Kennedy's caution clearly saved American lives during his presidency.

His experience standing up to military "experts" gave him a kind of confidence. He would have needed it if he chose to go against popular opinion over Vietnam. Johnson had no such reputation in foreign affairs. As vice president he usually sided with the advisers encouraging Kennedy to go to war.

Kennedy had been tested similarly before.

He had prevented the U.S. from getting involved in 1961 in Laos, another country in Southeast Asia. After France pulled out of Indochina, Laos and neighboring Cambodia were declared neutral countries. But a civil war soon broke out between the U.S.-supported government and the North Vietnamese-supported communist rebels. Kennedy had been encouraged by his advisers to send American troops, and some even suggested using nuclear weapons to prevent a communist takeover. Kennedy instead talked with Soviet Premier Nikita Khrushchev, and the two men agreed to a settlement. It was shaky, but it wasn't war.

Voters in 1964 would have had a clear choice. Kennedy would have been challenged by Barry Goldwater, an enthusiastic supporter of going to war in Vietnam. Given that choice and polling data from before the assassination, it seems the American people would probably have given Kennedy a second term. Nobody knows for sure. It's possible that Kennedy would have fulfilled a campaign promise of keeping the U.S. out of combat in Vietnam. Or he might have pursued the war but done so differently than Johnson did — for better or worse. Either way, the country might be a very different place today.

TIMELINE >>>>>>>>>>>>>>>>>>>>>>>>>

May 29, 1917: John F. Kennedy is born in Boston to Joseph and Rose Kennedy; he will be raised in prosperity and comfort

Oct. 18, 1939: Lee Harvey Oswald is born in Louisiana; he will be raised off and on by a single mother struggling for work who frequently uprooted the family

October 1941: Kennedy joins the U.S. Navy shortly before the U.S. enters World War II

Dec. 7, 1941: Japan attacks the American forces at Pearl Harbor, Hawaii, triggering the U.S. entry into World War II

Aug. 1, 1943: Kennedy's torpedo patrol boat, the PT-109, is rammed by a Japanese destroyer; after saving the lives of his men, Kennedy is hailed as a hero

Nov. 5, 1946: After his first political campaign, Kennedy is elected to the U.S. House of Representatives from the 11th District in Massachusetts

Nov. 4, 1952: Kennedy is elected to the U.S. Senate

May 7, 1954: Following a military defeat against the communist North Vietnamese at Dien Bien Phu, France surrenders control of Indochina (Vietnam, Laos, and Cambodia)

October 1956: Oswald joins the U.S. Marines; his training includes marksmanship

Jan. 1, 1959: Fidel Castro leads the overthrow of a military dictatorship in Cuba and establishes communist rule in the island nation

October 1959: Having been interested in communism and Marxism for years, Oswald seeks to become a citizen of the Soviet Union

Jan. 2, 1960: Kennedy announces his candidacy for U.S. president

July 1960: Delegates at the 1960 Democratic Convention in Los Angeles nominate Kennedy as the party's presidential candidate, with Lyndon B. Johnson as the candidate for vice president

Sept. 21, 1960: Kennedy and Republican candidate Richard M. Nixon take part in the first televised presidential debate

Nov. 8, 1960: Kennedy wins a narrow victory over Nixon

Jan. 20, 1961: Kennedy is sworn in as president of the United States

May 11, 1961: Following a strategy started by President Eisenhower, Kennedy sends 500 U.S. soldiers and advisers to South Vietnam

June 1962: Oswald, with his wife and child, returns from the Soviet Union to the United States

October 1962: The U.S. discovers that Cuba is building a missile base; Kennedy, amid calls for an invasion, establishes a blockade to confront the oncoming Soviet ships delivering missiles

Nov. 22, 1963: Oswald shoots and kills President Kennedy in Dallas

Nov. 23, 1963: Oswald is shot and killed by nightclub owner Jack Ruby

GLOSSARY

blockade—a military effort to keep goods from entering and leaving a region

Cold War—a conflict between the United States and the Soviet Union; although there was no direct fighting, the conflict lasted from about 1947 to 1990

communism—system in which goods and property are owned by the government and shared in common; communist rulers limit personal freedoms to achieve their goals

depository—a place where items are stored for safekeeping

embassy—building where the government representatives of another country work

Indochina—a peninsula in Southeast Asia, between India and China, containing Vietnam, Laos, Cambodia, Thailand, Myanmar, and the mainland territory of Malaysia.

Marxist—a person who believes in the theories of Karl Marx (considered the father of communism), who wrote that the struggles between rich and poor would be eliminated if there were no classes

militant—person who is aggressive or warlike in pursuing some cause or ideal

motorcade—group of cars or other motorized vehicles traveling together

patsy—a person who takes the blame for a crime, a scapegoat

socialism—an economic system in which the goods made by factories, businesses, and farms are controlled by the government

SOURCE NOTES

Page 20, line 16: Bugliosi, Vincent. *Reclaiming History: The Assassination of President John F. Kennedy*. New York: W.W. Norton & Company, Inc., 2007, p. 639.

Page 31, line 24: Dallek, Robert. *An Unfinished Life. John F. Kennedy 1917-1963*. New York: Black Bay Books/Little Brown and Company, 2003, p. 426.

Page 42, line 8: *Reclaiming History: The Assassination of President John F. Kennedy*, pp. 39-40.

Page 53, line 6: *An Unfinished Life. John F. Kennedy 1917-1963*, p. 450.

Page 54, line 10: Ibid, p. 458.

Page 55, line 9: Ibid, p. 686.

SELECT BIBLIOGRAPHY

Bugliosi, Vincent. *Reclaiming History: The Assassination of President John F. Kennedy*. New York: W.W. Norton & Company, Inc., 2007.

Blight, James G., Lang, Janet M., and Welch, David A. *Vietnam if Kennedy Had Lived: Virtual JFK*. Lanham, Md.: Rowman and Littlefield Publishers, 2009.

Caro, Robert. *The Passage of Power*. New York: Vintage Books, 2013.

Dallek, Robert. "JFK's Second Term." *The Atlantic*. June 2003.

Dallek, Robert. *An Unfinished Life. John F. Kennedy 1917-1963*. New York: Black Bay Books/Little Brown and Company, 2003.

Greenfield, Jeff. *If Kennedy Lived: The First and Second Terms of President John F. Kennedy: An Alternate History*. New York: G.P. Putnam's Sons, 2013.

Ridings Jr., William J. and Stuart B. McIver. *Rating the Presidents*. New York: Kensington Publishing Corp., 2000.

ADDITIONAL RESOURCES

READ MORE

Freedman, Russell. *Vietnam: A History of the War*. New York: Holiday House, 2016.

Nardo, Don. *Assassination and Its Aftermath*. North Mankato, Minn.: Compass Point Books, 2014.

Senker, Cath. *Kennedy and the Cuban Missile Crisis*. Chicago: Heinemann Library, 2014.

Swanson, James L. *The President Has Been Shot: The Assassination of John F. Kennedy*. New York: Scholastic Press, 2013.

INTERNET SITES

Use FactHound to find Internet sites related to this book.

Visit www.facthound.com

Just type in 9780756557133 and go.

INDEX

ABOUT THE AUTHOR

JOE TOUGAS

worked for 17 years as a daily newspaper reporter and editor and is the author of several books for young readers. He lives in North Mankato, Minnesota, and his website is joetougas.com.

PHOTO CREDITS

Getty Images: Bettmann, 53, Corbis, 14, 16, 24, Fotosearch, 18, Three Lions, 29; John F. Kennedy Library and Museum, 9; LBJ Library Photo by Frank Muto, 12; Library of Congress, cover, 4, 21, 30, 41, 55; Newscom: Everett Collection, 22, 42, 49, 51, Mondadori Portfolio, 44, Universal Images Group/Sovfoto, 26, Universal Images Group/ Underwood Archives, 33, UPI, 13, UPI/John F. Kennedy Presidential Library & Museum/Cecil Stoughton, 40, Zuma Press/JFK Collection, 47, Zuma Press/John F. Kennedy Library, 39, Zuma Press/Keystone Pictures USA, 7, Zuma Press/Keystone Press Agency, 11, Zuma Press/ Photoshot/Uppa, 48, Zuma Press/Photoshot/Uppa, 36

Design Elements by Shutterstock